DIVINE KARMA: THE CREATION

DAVID RAMIREZ

ISBN-13: 978-0-9983932-0-9

Divine Karma
P.O. Box 901147
Homestead, Florida 33090

www.Divine-Karma.com

DEDICATION

I dedicate this book to my family, friends, and those who've shared in my life experiences and have, unsuspectedly, helped me change my perspective and beliefs.

Most of all, I dedicate this book to myself. David, you have mustered the courage to change your perspective so that you could understand the fundamental nature of Self. Because of you, this book was created. Because of you, I was able to realize that all of my triumphs and failures were experiences created by me. I achieved a realization that I can now bring forth and share. You are a warrior and I honor your presence. Thank you.

CONTENTS

OUR STARTING POINT

In the beginning, before the curtain rose, there was us. We stood behind the curtain in darkness and we were nothing, yet we were everything. We were divine. But being divine, there was nothing for us to experience—there was no show. So we created a grand performance called *Life*, this existence we currently live in, and we became what is now 7 billion I's. We were no longer One. But there was no need to fret. Our story had just begun. We would unite again in the future and we would live in tune with our true nature. We knew that's how our story would end. All we needed to do was remember. Today is the first day of our journey to remembrance.

This is a guide for self-realization. You may have found it because you were searching for something meaningful in your life. Maybe you were just curious. Maybe it was a little bit of both. Whatever the reason for you finding it, and embarking on this journey with me, I thank you for showing up. We were meant to go on this quest together.

And so our journey begins here. Or it doesn't. The decision is yours to make. And the decision must be made on your own, without influence. Do not stay because you think I am a guru, teacher, or prophet. I am simply an investigator joining you on this path and serving as a guide during your exploration.

If you're wondering what led me here, it was a feeling. It was the feeling that everything I believed in my whole life was incorrect. I knocked on doors and explored the world in search for answers to some of the world's most fundamental, yet complex, questions: Who am I? Where am I? Why am I here? It dawned on me that I was going about it the wrong way. I was looking outside into the world before looking inside at myself. When I looked within, the search was over. But I knew the story was much bigger than that, much bigger than me. It was about all of us. It was about everyone discovering what lies within them and how society arrived at where it is today. We must investigate the things that have led up to this moment, and where we are to go from here. See, looking out into the world is actually a part of looking within because we're all connected. It's just about knowing where and how to look. And what to do with the information found. Which is why I couldn't help but welcome this opportunity for us to go on this journey and explore this mystery. I couldn't wait to realize my role in the show.

Our story may be simple, it may not be. It may take you an instant to understand, it may take your whole life. But you will come to understand it. Everyone will. We all have the opportunity to realize that we no longer have to live in conflict or confusion. Once we awaken to that, we can all evolve and live with a purpose of coexisting in a world free of suffering, attachments, and, most importantly, desire. This may sound utopian, but know that if we keep our eyes closed any longer then the world will remain in a perpetual state of chaos. In order to conduct a thorough investigation, we must look at some of the ideas and theories found within various bodies of knowledge. Thus, we will examine several sources including scientific studies as well as sacred texts found within various religions and spiritual sects. Doing so will give us a variety of perspectives and a greater, more concrete, understanding of what's being discussed. It will also lead us to the middle point, and we will see the truth of how we're all connected.

However, I do have one request. Do not bring your pre-conceived beliefs with you on this journey. Put aside your interpretations and opinions concerning the subjects of religion, science, and spirituality. This will allow you to look at and analyze the information without automatically dismissing it because it doesn't fit into one of your current ingrained beliefs.

As humans, we tend to solely acknowledge and believe the things that fit into our pre-conceived definition of how we view and interpret the world. However, only when we start questioning everything can we realize that most of the concepts we've come to believe were either heavily misguided, misinterpreted, or incomplete. This can be a difficult task in practice and is often hard to accept because most of what we've learned was taught to us, and continuously instilled in us, by our trusted elders that came before us. Otherwise, we may have never believed them. Or we would've questioned them.

It isn't my objective to dismiss or disprove the things you've learned from your parents, siblings, friends, community, a lecturer, a teacher, or even what you've read or watched yourself. I just ask that you question it.

Questioning is essential to this process—honest and authentic questioning. I implore you, question everything within these pages. I wouldn't want you to believe it just because it was written and published. I don't want you to believe anything that's been told to you. That way of thinking is the root of all of our conflict and how we ended up in the state we're in now. It is imperative that we let go of that behavior and open our minds to other possibilities and perspectives. Opening your mind is the first step. Then, begin to question, examine, and test everything you think you know. Allow yourself to acknowledge the beliefs that are actually yours versus those you inherited.

There are two ways to test where your beliefs and understandings came from: direct observation and indirect observation. A direct observation is something that you observe using one or more of your physical senses (i.e. sight, sound, touch, taste, smell). For example, you can directly observe the flame of a fire as being hot. An indirect observation, on the other hand, is something you read about or learn through the use of a tool, such as a telescope or camera lens. So while you directly observe the flame of a fire as being hot, if you indirectly observe the fire via a photograph of it you will only perceive the visual image and not its heat. Regardless of your means of testing, the truth is that both kinds of observations should be questioned. In doing so, you will plant the seed in your mind to question all things you encounter and you will be able to better discern the conclusions you've arrived at yourself versus the theories and conclusions of others. You will also have a broader perspective of the experience.

I must also impart that it isn't my objective to give you a new belief system either. We're not breeding followers here. All I'm doing is joining you as you explore your mind and realize all of the knowledge within you. This is your opportunity to investigate yourself. Be a detective. Realize everything inside of you, inside of the entire world, and how wonderfully intricate it all is.

This is your opportunity to better understand who you are, what's going around you, and what that means for your life. This book is a catalyst that will open your heart and mind in a variety of ways that, while inevitably raise questions, will unlock a greater and more in-depth awareness of the world. And with it, you can live with purpose. You can live a life in harmony with yourself. When you finish this book, you'll know what to do.

EFFECTIVE METHODS OF QUESTIONING

There are several methods of questioning from various schools of thought that you can use while on our journey. Below are some of the ones I have found to be most effective, along with some valuable conclusions that can be used to question and figure out the truth as well.

The famous philosopher Socrates, for example, understood that truth was of the highest value and that it could only be discovered through reason and logic. By way of reasoned arguments, in which one contradicts a thesis by producing an antithesis, can one arrive at an ultimate synthesis. The Hegelian Dialectic Method, named after Georg Wilhelm Friedrich Hegel, follows a similar pattern: an opinion or idea is presented as thesis, gives rise to a reaction known as the antithesis that contradicts or negates the thesis, which is then resolved by means of a synthesis. This method has no end, for the synthesis would simply become the new thesis and the process would continue over and over again, as in a helix. The ultimate goal is to find an absolute synthesis, to determine what is without question.

Nagarjuna was a teacher and Buddhist philosopher who lived in the second century. He used the dialectic method in his discourses as well.

Following it, he came to the logical conclusion that "All things exist; All things do not exist; All things both exist and do not exist; All things neither exist nor do not exist."

But questioning, in reality and in practice, goes a step beyond the testing used in the Hegelian method. There's a human factor that goes deeper, past the surface: thought. Thought is what both initiates and ultimately completes the test.

René Descartes, a French philosopher, mathematician, and scientist that lived in the early seventeenth century, is famous for the saying *Cogito ergo sum*, meaning, "I think, therefore I am." Such primal and powerful words. But in my opinion, his more memorable quote should be: "If you would be a real seeker after truth, it is necessary that at least once in your life you doubt, as far as possible, all things." Descartes was the progenitor of modern philosophy and established that, in order to determine truth, we must question everything we've learned and experienced. After such questioning, then we can accept that which is unquestionable.

Siddhartha Gautama, otherwise known as the Buddha, knew and practiced this principle as well. He advised, "Don't go by reports, by legends, by traditions, by scripture, by logical conjecture, by inference, by analogies, by agreement through pondering views, by probability, or by the thought, 'This contemplative is our teacher.' When you know for yourselves that, 'These qualities are skillful; these qualities are blameless; these qualities are praised by the wise; these qualities, when adopted

& carried out, lead to welfare & to happiness' —
then you should enter & remain in them."

So now here's a question: Does God exist?
If we utilize the conclusion discovered by
Nagarjuna, this is what we find: "God exists; God
does not exist; God both exists and does not exist;
God neither exists nor does not exist." What would
Socrates conclude? I wonder. Using his methods, he
probably wouldn't even give an answer but ask
another question. "Well, does God not exist?" We
can then channel Descartes and say, "Who is God?
What, or who, created God? Why do I care about
God's existence, anyway? I'm not sure what I think,
but I will ruminate, I will doubt, and I will find
out." And heeding Buddha's advice we will declare,
"I will not go by what others tell me. I will think for
myself what the nature of God is, and whether or

not I believe he exists. And what it would mean for my life if he did."

We are ultimately brought to the conclusion that whether or not God exists is based on our belief of whether or not he does, and our belief in the method used to discover that truth. When really, at the end of it all, God is just a concept. It does not matter if God exists or doesn't. And only if you have an investment in the belief that he does, will God exist and have an influence in your life.

Although I by no means want to limit you to these, understanding the aforementioned methods of questioning, and how to use them to analyze your beliefs and what you've come to know, will allow you to reach a realization that asserts the true nature of your reality. Doing so is vital to your results and growth as you read this book.

PART ONE

THE COLLECTIVE CONSCIOUSNESS

WHAT IS THE COLLECTIVE?

The collective consciousness is the bond that unites all of our experiences and the endless possibilities thereof. It is the unifying energy that sustains the world. Occurrences and experiences of the past, present, and future, in varying forms and degrees, are all within it. It is a repository that contains everything there is to know about the world, and is accessible to everyone.

It is the space from which we retrieve information or experiences using our senses, thoughts, and feelings, in order to make decisions and know how to react to something we've never personally experienced before. It is the script that dictates how we should act. Because of this information, for example, we know that touching something hot will burn us and drinking something deemed poisonous will harm us. The collective consciousness is what forms our intuition. Thus, to be guided by our intuition, is to be actively connected to the collective.

The collective consciousness is a living, ever-evolving source. It evolves with the times. So whatever is being experienced by individuals in a certain period of time, is how the general population of that time is going to behave. It supports the beliefs of all conscious beings, for it contains what people are aware of in that time. Therefore, what was in the collective consciousness during prehistoric times, or even during the Renaissance, was vastly different from what's in our awareness right now. It changes as we change. It evolves as we do. So whatever we subscribe to, the collective consciousness will support and will create our environment accordingly. Whatever we love or hate, brave or fear, construct or destruct, will be manifested in our collective minds and the environment. Rest assured, the collective will look very different in the mind of someone who reads these words a hundred years from now.

HIVE MIND

The collective consciousness grows in conjunction with our minds. So as our minds grow and expand, so does the collective consciousness. Consider the 100th monkey phenomenon, for instance. In 1952, an experiment was conducted on the Japanese island of Koshima. Scientists dropped sweet potatoes onto the sand and observed the native monkeys as they ate them. Although the sweet potato was pleasant, the sand proved to be very problematic. One monkey, an infant named Imo, eventually solved the problem by washing her potato in a nearby stream. She then taught her mother. Subsequently, more and more monkeys began to learn this skill until all of the monkeys on the island knew how to wash their sweet potatoes in the stream. That was a wonder on its own. But it wasn't until some time later that the most interesting phenomenon occurred. Monkeys on a nearby island, ones that had no communication with the monkeys on Koshima, also began to wash their potatoes in a similar manner without being taught to do so. How was that possible? These islands were separated by the ocean with no possibility of a monkey traveling from one island to the other. If we think about how the collective works, we can conclude that when all of the monkeys on Koshima learned to wash their potatoes to remove the sand, they reached a critical mass and began to harmonize their consciousness with the consciousness of the other monkeys far away. Thus, the awareness wasn't just apparent on the one island, but became the norm for both. This is how behaviors become well known and, even, expected.

This phenomenon can also be seen and understood using random number generators (RNGs). For fifteen years, starting in 1998, the Global Consciousness Project combined science and engineering to study the possible interaction of a global consciousness with the physical world. They set up random number generating machines in around seventy sites around the globe that collected data continuously. The purpose was to examine subtle correlations that would reflect the presence of a collective consciousness, as well as its activity. They hypothesized that the random data wouldn't be random at all. They believed there would be structure in the data, patterns, during times of major global events. This was proven to be true, and quite evident, just before the attacks on September 11, 2001. What was considered a statistical anomaly proved to be data consistent with the time and general location of the terrorist attacks on 9/11. It was as if we were all aware that the event was going to happen, before it did. Or, rather, if we think about the effects of the collective consciousness on our environment, enough people thought of something similar that then created the supporting environment to manifest the event. Considering this, it's probably no coincidence that the winning numbers for the New York State Lottery were 9-1-1 on September 11, 2002, when the events of 9-11 were on the minds of most, if not all, New Yorkers on its first anniversary.

These examples support the theory of not only the presence of a collective consciousness, but also how a hive mind works. They offer insight into how our minds function both individually and in unison.

NATURE'S ROLE

Nature plays a significant role in the evolution of the collective consciousness. In this performance, nature is our director. As the collective consciousness evolves, nature will work with the collective to support the environment desired, but it will also keep everything in balance to ensure the show goes on. For example, when humans cut down forests, nature ensures that the seeds of the trees fall to the ground and begin to grow new ones. Sometimes this phenomenon is slow in time, but nature always acts.

Look at what happened at Chernobyl. In April 1986, an explosion occurred at the Chernobyl Nuclear Power Plant in Ukraine that released large quantities of radioactive isotopes into the atmosphere. Consequently, the area surrounding the plant was found to be unsuitable for human life and there was a mass evacuation of over 115,000 people. This thirty-kilometer exclusion area surrounding the nuclear plant was labeled the "zone of alienation." Though the leak had and has been contained, it is still uninhabited and off-limits with the exception of some residents who have returned and refused to leave. That being said, the most interesting thing occurred when nature stepped in. The forests nearby became a unique wildlife sanctuary even though scientific assessments had declared that the area could not support a vibrant growth in nature after such a catastrophic event. In this instance, we can perfectly see how nature brings balance to the world. And it always will—no matter how difficult or impossible it may seem.

PART TWO

THE HUMAN EXPERIENCE

AN INDIVIDUAL EXPRESSION

Each individual human experience is a unique expression of the collective. Your life is the individual perspective you wish to experience in the performance. We are all in the same play, just portraying different roles. And each role contributes to the collective. This means that the actions we take towards others have an effect on the collective. Ultimately, that means that what we do to others in turn gets done to us, as that old saying goes. Yet we perceive ourselves as separate. If we, for a moment, think of ourselves as one and the same, we would act differently. In order to reach that sense of community and sameness, however ironically, we must investigate that which makes our human experience unique: the mind.

THE HUMAN MIND

Our minds are what create our thoughts, and our thoughts are what create our reality. Thoughts are what our bodies use to breathe, to make our hearts beat, to experience taste, see colors, sense smell, feel hardness, and hear sounds. We cannot engage the world without thought—it is a necessity in order to interact with it. And our senses play a very important role in how our thoughts are created. Our senses are the tools we created to gauge the world around us—the world we deem real. So because our thoughts are an integral part of how we experience life, it is crucial that we understand how different aspects of our minds function. We must analyze some of the underlying causes that create the thoughts in our minds.

In 1927, Romain Rolland coined the phrase "oceanic feeling." The term referred to the sensation of feeling eternal and without perceptible limits, like the ocean. But it wasn't popularized until Sigmund Freud, an Austrian neurologist and the founder of Psychoanalysis, analyzed its effect on our lives. "Oceanic feeling" describes the connectedness of an infant to its mother and its inability to differentiate itself as independent from its mother, for example. This phenomenon occurs most prevalently in the pre-ego stage of development when an infant has not yet grasped the concept of self as being separate from others. This is an awareness we all had at birth. However, as our personalities developed and we matured, the ego also developed and became involved in our everyday lives.

What's interesting is that it seems as though we still sense or crave that "oceanic feeling," whether we're consciously aware of it or not. Freud noticed this and theorized that, as adults, we would covet certain groups of people, mainly in religious groups in which one seeks the psychological phenomena of oneness with each other, which is common in our world. So it is clear that a part of us strives for that oneness once more.

That being said, as a pioneer in studying how humans achieve their individuality, Freud also analyzed and defined the structural model of our personalities for us. According to him, our behaviors are the outcome of the interactions between the following three components: the id, the ego, and the superego.

The id is the instinctive, primitive, part of us that operates according to the pleasure principle. It demands the instant gratification of its urges. The id is what also houses our biological urges such as the desire to eat, sleep, and have sex.

The ego plays a key role in our decision-making, as it operates according to the reality principle, and delays the id's urges until conditions are suitable. The ego then mediates between the id and the external world, between the id and society. The ego considers societal norms, behaviors, and rules. Being realistic, the ego strives to avoid negative consequences from society. In a way, while it keeps us protected from possible harm of venturing into what is "taboo" or unknown, it also keeps us conformed. It sets a limitation on our goals and desires.

Finally, we have the superego. The superego is what houses our morale. It considers social standards about what is right and wrong, as often learned by our parents and teachers.

Each of us, depending on our environment, will have different ids, egos, and superegos. Because of this environmental and cultural difference, our behaviors are unique. Hence, how our experiences are individual and unique expressions.

Furthermore, we must highlight how the ego uses individual thought to make sense of reality. It is the unique mask we wear in order to engage in the world. And again, the ego is what makes sure that your goals are realistic and achievable, ensuring that the id does not allow you to create unrealistic expectations. For example, if you're watching a movie and the main character dodges an arrow, your id may identify with the character's natural and instinctive ability and you may suddenly want to try to dodge an arrow yourself. Immediately, the ego will step in and present you will all related limitations so that you never try such a dangerous trick, which, according to the superego, is unacceptable behavior. This way of thinking keeps us limited and stops us from daring to try new things, experiences that may be possible if we would believe.

If we are to transcend this way of thinking, we will need to transform our dependency on the limitations set by our ids, egos, and superegos. These limitations are simply constructs created by society and serve only to maintain strength in our beliefs. In order to begin this transformation, we will need to become aware of our perceived limitations.

Consider those three components and look at your life. What are some of the primal urges and cravings you have or have had? Did you satisfy them instantly? If not, what stopped you? What thoughts occurred that delayed your gratification or even denied it completely? Was it a particular societal standard? If so, where did it come from? Did you arrive at that judgment from your own experiences? Or was it based on a belief that was passed down to you by a parent or other advisor? Think about it. When you arrive at the conclusion, ask yourself if you still have that initial urge. You may find that it disappears altogether. Or you may find that the urge still occurs, but is no longer a thought in your mind if you should do it. You just do.

If you want to further test your limitations, have someone you trust prepare various food items for you to try without them telling you what they've made. When you're sitting and ready, place a blindfold over your eyes, plug your nose, and have them place one food item into your mouth without describing the item to you. There will be a high probability that you will be unable to determine the exact consistency and flavor. But, the taste buds on your tongue may be able to determine some of the items using a process of elimination. This test reflects how our senses can and will work together to ensure that the program that has already exists and what you're experiencing in the moment does not conflict. So frog legs will inevitably taste like chicken because chicken is the most commonly used program and is known to everyone in the collective.

KARMA

In Buddhism, the Second Noble Truth states that desire is the cause of suffering. And desire is the root of attachment. Thus, Buddha taught that liberation from desire and, subsequently, attachment can only come by following the Middle Way. The Middle Way, or Middle Path, is a lifestyle where there is no attachment to anything. There are no sides. There is a sense of neutrality because no judgment is placed on any part of an experience. When in the Middle, one is living in their true and natural state.

Should you dwell in any state other than your natural state, have any desires or attachments, you will create karma. Karma is derived from the Sanskrit word *karman* which means "action." The way it works is that when you seek something an imbalance is created because there is a dualistic component to all things. So when you decide to act in one direction, karma will present the other. In order for you to have the opportunity to be brought back into balance, karma brings that conflict to the forefront so that it may be released.

Picture a scale. As you place a desire, or an emotional attachment to an experience, on one of the pans, you will inevitably tip the scale and create an imbalance. It is not the actual thing you desire that tips the scale, it's the seeking of it. To seek is to act out of your natural state. It is when the ego and superego come into play and make a decision. To be in your natural state is to be more in tune with your id, in a way. The idea is for there not to be any thought to your actions, but to do as your nature wills without your influence.

BALANCE OF EMOTIONS

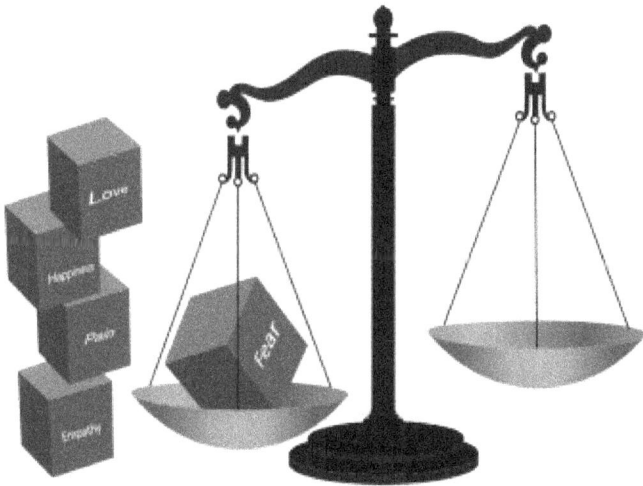

So, in order to bring the scale back to balance, you will need to release the desire. And you will need to release any emotional attachment to the experience. The karma will, consequently, be released as well. Otherwise, you will create what is known as "karmic debt." If there is ever a karmic debt for your actions, know that those same actions, or similar experiences, will keep appearing until the karma is "paid."

To reiterate, our existence in this reality is infused with many experiences that we have the ability to infuse emotional attachment to. When you attach yourself to an experience, you create karma that will inevitably need to be released in order to be brought to balance once again. To be brought back to balance and understand these principles is fundamental to becoming aware and being in harmony with all of your experiences.

Once that harmony is achieved and you are released from the karmic cycle, you will be liberated from the ties that have kept you enslaved.

This liberation expands your awareness and allows you to observe all things as they are without dwelling in any experience. To be liberated in this way is to have reached salvation. The Sanskrit word for this is *Nirvana* or *Moksha*, meaning "liberation and release." In other words, "breathe out and let go.

Everyone in this existence has his or her own karma. These karmic interactions create our world. It is another one of the ways we are all connected. But our connection is truly more than that. When we realize that we're not just connected but are one and the same, we will come full circle and be in tune with the collective once more. And we will be consciously aware of it.

PART THREE

THE TRINITY OF TRUTH

WHAT IS IT?

The Trinity of Truth is a construct of the human mind. It is a triangle uniting religion, science, and spirituality. Within this triangle is the truth, the understanding of humanity and life on Earth. With it, you can either use it to actualize a deeper connection to your divine self which will lead you to a life in tune with the collective, or remain connected and bound to the illusion of your individual human experience.

Everyone in the world, by design, perceives reality through one or more of the three disciplines that makes up the Trinity. These branches of knowledge shape our beliefs. The mistake we often make, however, is thinking that they are separate entities that do not intersect. We believe that they actually oppose each other. Well, while each may have their own methods of teaching and a varied body of knowledge that is explored, they actually do intersect and meet in the middle.

TRINITY OF TRUTH

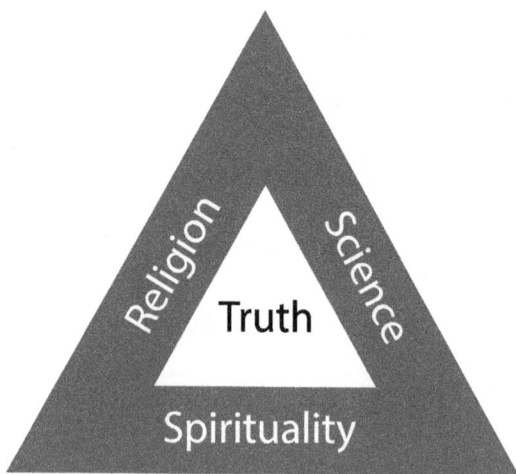

There is truth in each of the realms. Everyone is right. Still, we have held fast to the belief that everyone is different, and that we must choose the beliefs we subscribe to and deny those of others. For ages, this perceived separation has had us at war with each other, with the environment, and with ourselves. We are constantly fighting each other, destroying nature, putting up walls, and judging and discriminating against one another. If one would look deeper, one would find that there is no actual separation. Separation is an illusion we created ourselves—in our minds.

There is at least one all-encompassing truth that is supported by all the realms, a truth that unites all of humankind: we were all created by one source, by the same source. There have been many names for this source: Universe, Creator, Source, and, most often, God. Now whether you believe God to be a man or a ball of energy makes no difference. There is no arguing that some unifying source created the world and everything in it. Something cannot be created from nothing. And this source is the only one that exists. It is the only one that there has ever been and will ever be.

Up to now, I've asked that you question everything being discussed. And I ask that you continue doing so. But this one awareness is the most crucial to your growth. This is a talisman for you to retrieve at this point in the story and hold on to for the rest. Keep this, and all else will make sense.

Once you understand that there is only one source and that we all came from it, you will begin to understand what that truth means as it pertains to all the realms, and how that truth functions to sustain the world we live in. And when you actualize and embody it, your conscious awareness will shift. Collectively, this will cause a ripple effect through the entire world. It will raise our individual awareness to form a more unified collective consciousness.

There are breadcrumbs that can be found anywhere and everywhere that show the truth of the Trinity, breadcrumbs that point to more clues to the mystery of our lives, breadcrumbs from all three bodies of knowledge. When we find them and further see the correlation between the three ideologies, we can utilize its power to uncover who we are and what our purpose in life is. If you just take these beliefs at face value, based on what others have interpreted rather than your own testing or questioning, then you won't see the truth past the surface. So when conducting your investigation and searching for answers, you must observe the world without any filters. Otherwise, you won't be able to objectively question everything you're experiencing and will not become aware of the truth being revealed.

It is important to highlight that without having questioned all of your current beliefs, your reality is based on faith in what you've accepted blindly. In order to maintain power and dominion over the masses, leaders need only create a dogmatic fear, a belief that supports that fear, and then subjugate those who don't support those beliefs. And if that doesn't work, persecute, ridicule, and then ostracize anyone who challenges those beliefs so that they don't infect the fearful with their knowledge. Not suggesting a conspiracy here, but I am suggesting that maybe power originated by someone or a group of people who were trying to guide others through treacherous and difficult times, and the only way to ensure their cooperation and safety was to provide a convincing belief that supported a purported fear. And as this scenario evolved, people no longer wanted to stray from the herd and found comfort in such beliefs. Anyone who didn't subscribe to those beliefs was cast away and vilified by those that wouldn't allow a rogue non-believer to destroy their comfortable and unquestioned beliefs.

To follow blindly is to follow in fear. It's time to be fearless. And to discover that there's nothing to fear. There never has been.

RELIGION

By definition, religion is "a cause, principle, or system of beliefs held to with order and faith." More specifically, it's the realm that studies the cause, nature, and purpose of our existence, which is considered to be the creation of a superhuman agency or agencies. Religion usually involves devotional and ritual observances, and contains a moral code that governs the conduct of human affairs.

Religion, in many cases, is also a social institution, as in organized religion. In organized religion, beliefs and rituals are arranged and formally established in the community. Within this kind, there is an official bureaucratic leadership that governs it. The term "organized religion" is used by the media to refer to the world's largest religious groups, especially those known by name internationally, which one can legally or officially affiliate oneself with.

When I speak of religion, I am primarily referring to those organized religions that fall under the Abrahamic, East Asian, and Indian faiths. To me, religions encompass the belief systems that focus on a reward that is obtained in the afterlife, or after this life. It is a way of paving one's steps in life by thinking of what's to come after one passes, based on one's actions while alive.

Part of paving those steps in life is comparing our own actions to those featured in religious texts, such as the Bible. The stories we read heavily influence the things we do and what we constitute as right or wrong. I've noticed, however, that faith in these texts and stories is often blind, for it entails being obedient without question in order to receive God's approval and grace which determines the reward you will receive in the afterlife. If merited, of course.

That being said, religion holds much wisdom, especially regarding who we are. Let's look at some verses and scriptures, and review their message. Let's dissect them. Let's see what pieces we can put together.

THE DIVINITY THAT LIVES WITHIN

The Bible is one of the most followed texts on Earth, divulging valuable information that has guided humanity for two millennia. It is also one of the most misunderstood texts in history, often repeating the same message in various verses yet completely escaping its followers. For example, the Bible reveals one of the most essential truths about mankind. In black and white, it unveils the truth that we were made in God's image. We are divine and like God. That means that we possess all of the powers of creation. We created the world and everything in it. We are God.

I know what you must be thinking. Did I really just say that? Yes, I did. You may reread "We are God" and think that I'm out of my mind, just another blasphemous fool who thinks that God and man are one and the same. It's okay if you think that. But before you take that as a reason to toss this book into the trash, let me show you what I mean.

In the King James Version of the Bible, in Luke 17:21, it reads, "The kingdom of God is within you" (Luke 17:21, KJV). While some later versions have re-translated it to read, "The kingdom of God is among you" (Luke 17:21, NLT) or "in the midst of you" (Luke 17:21, ESV). I want us to focus on that original version. On second thought, let's look at all three. If you think about it, if one is true, then all must be true. If God is within you, then he must be within everyone around you, meaning he is among you, and within every living being. Him being among us means that his energy, his essence and form, is omnipresent in our lives and the Earth around us. As an energy that is omnipresent, one can conclude that to be present everywhere means not only present externally but present internally as well. And the qualities we possess inside of us make us who we are. We cannot distinguish the creation from its creator—whatever is created is a direct product of the creator and possesses all of its qualities. So it is clear that each of us has God inside. Each of us is God. This truth has been hard for most to understand and, much less, accept.

ADAM AND EVE, AND THE BIRTH OF
DUALITY

The story of Creation, as written in the
Bible, is one that can shed some light as to why the
above truth was lost to us and is not such a
commonly held belief.

According to Genesis 1:1, "In the beginning,
God created the heavens and the Earth" (Genesis
1:1, ESV). He then created the sea and land, night
and day, and creatures to roam. All of his creations
came in pairs, in opposites—a hint that duality was
a part of creation, apparent since the start.

Then, man was created. However, at first,
there was only Adam. Eve came later on. How
could this be?

In Genesis Rabbah 8:5 of the Jewish
Midrash Rabbah, it reads, "What did the Lord do?

He took Truth and cast it to the ground... Let Truth spring up from the earth." Adam was created from absolute truth. He knew he was one with the divine source. However, God knew that this could not remain—Adam needed to have an opposite. God said it himself. In Genesis 2:18, God said, "It is not good that the man should be alone; I will make him a helper fit for him" (Genesis 2:18, RSV). Eve was then created from "his side." She was created to contrast, or complement, Adam. Thus, she was created using the same source, meaning she needed to have come from Adam. Eve was that helper that made Adam "good." In the Old Testament, the Hebrew translation of the word *ezer kenegdo* refers to a helper that opposes. Therefore, we can conclude that Eve was created to be Adam's alter ego. So, when the serpent tempts Eve, it is actually

Adam's alter ego that succumbs and eats the fruit from The Tree of Knowledge. Adam was never tempted to eat from The Tree of Knowledge before Eve. Due to the presence of Adam's alter ego, embodied as Eve, they ate from The Tree and became human. This event was the moment man disconnected from and forgot his divine nature. The notion that we were like God was lost to us from that moment on.

Adam and Eve are the metaphors used to describe our consciousness, the creation of the ego and separation from the divine spark. Remember, as Genesis 1:27 reads, "So God created mankind in his own image, in the image of God he created him; male and female he created them" (Genesis 1:27, ESV). This was how it was in the beginning until we "fell."

Many philosophers and artists have explored a similar idea before, but weren't taken very seriously. We never heard more about it, anyway. Take Michelangelo, the famous Italian sculptor and painter, for instance. In the early 1500s, Michelangelo painted a fresco in the Sistine Chapel called the *Creation of Adam.* In this fresco, God appears to be reaching to Adam, his creation. But, as physician Frank Meshberger, MD, noted one day as he toured the chapel, the red shroud surrounding God and his angels looks like the anatomical outline of the human brain. Another observation is that Eve was painted under the left arm of God observing Adam. Why was she not depicted beside him? Even more intriguing, Adam is drawn with a navel, which would suggest that Adam was born from a womb and not created. Adam born? Of whom? What would that mean if it were true?

(*The Creation of Adam* Illustration: www.iStock.com/tonybaggett)

In the painting, Michelangelo portrayed Eve in the recesses of the mind, as the alter ego. Since God had created Adam in his image and Eve was in Adam's mind, it shows us that the concept of duality between ego and alter ego is represented in the masculinity and femininity inside all of us. Through this concept of duality, it can be seen how God extracted the feminine from the masculine to create two from one. The ego and the alter ego were complementary to each other and neither could exist without the other. The most important message here is that they were one.

THE POWER TO FORGE THE LIGHT AND THE DARK

Again, God created everything. If you understand that you are God, then you know that you are a creator too. What do you create? Well, let's take a look at what God creates.

In the book of Isaiah 45:7, are the words "I form the light, and create darkness: I make peace, and I create evil: I the LORD do all these things" (Isaiah 45:7, KJV). So, from that line, it can be understood that God created both good and evil. This follows the same duality construct that was established when the Earth was created. Therefore, as you may have guessed, this means that you create both good and evil as well. This is the very power, the very energy, that creates the world we perceive and what is considered good or evil. Our beliefs are what support this perception. And religious texts have been crucial to what those perceptions and opinions are.

Every religion has a means for showing both sides. They have God, or a series of gods, and The Devil. But what they don't tell you is that God and The Devil, like good and evil, both live inside of us. Both must exist, that's just how duality works. The issue is when we cling to either side and create an opinion or judgment of it.

Our minds create thoughts, and thoughts create reality based on our beliefs and perceptions. Thoughts also create judgments of the reality we're experiencing, leading to those "good" or "bad" thoughts. In reality, the idea is to not pick any side but to realize the two sides are of one coin. Forget sides and focus on the coin. If you understand this, you will be able to look at your life, and the things that happen to you, differently.

Think of something, a person, or situation that you perceive as being "bad." Now, try to think of how that "bad" thing is actually "good." Is there a lesson to be learned? Seeing the greater picture will allow you to understand "the coin," how it works, and how you can begin to become less attached to something and be able to see it for all that it is. Everything we perceive has its duality, if not we would be unable to infuse an opinion or judgment about what we perceived. In other words, if you find something to be good or bad, black or white, up or down, or left or right, each has its alter ego, which is the opposing force that complements the original, and the only thing that separates them is your judgment, belief, or opinion.

For example, say you get divorced from the person that may have been challenging, but meant everything to you. You'd most likely see it as a bad experience. However, because you are now divorced, you find a person that you easily fall in love with, someone who accepts your strengths as well as your weaknesses. This opportunity manifested itself when and the way it did because of the first relationship. Because of the first, you were able to appreciate the relationship that came after. This new person may even be your soul mate. Everything happens for a reason. The reason eludes us when we're attached to either side of the coin and don't allow ourselves to see the whole picture.

OUR LIFE'S PURPOSE

According to some understandings found in religion, you are to fear the Creator who will judge you for your faith and duty, or lack thereof. This notion, this agenda, has many believing that this is our ultimate fate, to be judged by the Creator and either be rewarded or punished in the afterlife. But it is just that, an agenda. As we can see now, it is not the entire truth. You have a duty, but it's not to an outside source. The duty is to yourself. And there is no need to fear.

Seeing that we started as divine but lost our way, it would only seem right that our only purpose would be to get back on that path and live in tune with our divine nature once more.

Mystics of various major religions knew that this was our cause, and they knew how to achieve it. Original writings reveal a path in which the follower could guide himself to find union with self, with God. It is in this journey that we are able to navigate through the complexity of our perceptions and beliefs that leads us to a rebirth of our true self as we become one with God.

Chief Luther Standing Bear, an Oglala Lakota Native American, said, "The Indian loved to worship. From birth to death, he revered his surroundings. He considered himself born in the luxurious lap of Mother Earth, and no place was to him humble. There was nothing between him and the Big Holy (Wakan Tanka). The contact was immediate and personal, and the blessings of Wakan Tanka flowed over the Indian like rain showered from the sky. Wakan Tanka was not aloof, apart, and ever seeking to quell evil forces. He did not punish the animals and the birds, and likewise, he did not punish man. He was not a punishing god. For there was never a question as to the supremacy of an evil power over and above the power of Good. There was but one ruling power, and that was Good."

SCIENCE

Science is the "systematic knowledge of the physical or material world gained through observation and experimentation." It is the study of the natural and physical world, both its structure and behavior, in which knowledge is obtained by observing it carefully and experimenting. What I'm referring to, in particular, is Newtonian Physics. Most scientists have taken a worldview in support of Newtonian physics where matter is made up of cells and atoms. Their view is that nature and the universe are mechanical and can be controlled. We have a role in controlling it.

The most fundamental rule of science, and the biggest tool in its arsenal, is that the knowledge it presents is based on ideas that have been proven and tested. Although sometimes there may be ambiguity in the findings of an experiment, the information presented holds great weight and is considered to be credible because it can be replicated. And what serves as the means for this credibility is the level of questioning that is involved in the scientific method.

The Scientific Method is crucial. It demonstrates how we should look at experiences and information. We must hypothesize, test, experiment, question. There's a lot to be learned from science and its impact on us as well as the understanding of our lives. That is why I decided to include some well-known scientific experiments and findings in our investigation. These studies will help us elaborate on our human nature and the environment we live in. It is your task, as has been expected behavior throughout, to consider and question the information that is presented. Let's see if our beliefs and what we know can stand up to such scrutiny.

OUR THOUGHTS CREATE OUR REALITY

Scientists estimate that there are trillions of microorganisms in the human body, and declare that those organisms cannot live without you. Therefore, you are their creator.

From where science is capable of proving, all matter, us included, is molecularly created from atoms, and these atoms are comprised of protons, which have positive charge and electrons, which have negative charge. They are opposites that are attracted to each other. When these atoms are balanced, they will have the same amount of protons and electrons. Therefore, an atom when balanced will create energy. This is observable when using an electric plug on an appliance. The only way the appliance can function is only when both the negative and positive charge are connected, creating the power to turn it on.

Thus, all experiences that include matter are created by atoms existing in a form of balance. Nature is in constant balance and it's our perception that creates the imbalance in how we observe nature. When you observe a fire in a forest, you may perceive it as destruction, but nature sees cleansing and rebirth of a new forest. The perception may differ, but the action is the same. There is a fire.

Furthermore, you have a physical body that lives in a physical world, and this physical world is comprised of many physical, tangible, things. This is what you know and understand, that we live in a material world. But scientists have conducted numerous experiments, including the Double-slit Experiment, which have resulted in the understanding that only when there was an observer could matter exist—otherwise everything is formed as a wave, as in light and sound, as opposed to a particle. In reality, the world is made up entirely of wave patterns. But upon you observing it, is the world materialized. Therefore, when you open your senses, your eyes for instance, you are directly creating the world you are observing—you are what's bringing it into existence. And these creations you are observing are all based on your beliefs and perceptions of the pre-conceived constructs and observations found within the collective consciousness. This is a very simplistic summary of the experiment, but it has been tested and, using variations of these experiments, we have learned a great deal about how things function and what that means for our lives.

Since science has dissected our reality to reveal that everything is made of atoms, and until there's an observer the material world does not exist, that means that the only knowledge we can prove is the knowledge we've gathered from our own observations. Anything else is simply an idea that can't be proven, making it dismissible. Although our observations can be deceiving, we should always question what we do not directly observe.

Participatory Anthropic Principle, which was first proposed by Dr. John Wheeler, an eminent theoretical physicist, determined that without observers there could be no reality. Therefore, consciousness literally creates the physical world. In Wheeler's Delayed-choice Experiment, he concluded that the attempt to detect a photon after passing through the double-slit would interfere and change the outcome of the experiment and its behavior.

Dr. Bruce Lipton is a cellular biologist who also experimented with the idea that our thoughts affect us and our world. He proposed that our genes and DNA are manipulated by our beliefs. In his research, he concluded that cells would adapt to whatever environment was present in a petri dish. Dr. Lipton, when studying cells adapting to its environment in a petri dish, said, "I realized that a cell's life is fundamentally controlled by the physical and energetic environment with only a small contribution by its genes. Genes are simply molecular blueprints used in the construction of cells, tissues, and organs. The environment serves as a 'contractor' who reads and engages those genetic blueprints and is ultimately responsible for the character of a cell's life. It is a simple cell's 'awareness' of the environment that sets into motion the mechanisms of life."

The English geologist and naturalist, Charles Darwin, had concluded in his theory of evolution that natural selection was nature's method to randomly mutate genes that were beneficial to the development of the species, and thus were passed on from generation to generation, and continued evolving in order for the species to survive and reproduce. However, Jean-Baptiste Lamarck, a French naturalist, had theorized that evolution was an inheritance of acquired characteristics and that organisms evolved while adapting to their environment. These two theorists have proposed valid supported arguments that have led to the dichotomous debate of Nature vs. Nurture. However, most scientists now believe that an organism's development is conditional and can be attributed to both nurture and nature.

C.H. Waddington, an embryologist and renowned biologist, wrote in 1957, "It is of course a truism which has been long recognised that the development of any individual is affected both by the hereditary determinants which come into the fertilised egg from the two parents and also by the nature of the environment in which the development takes place." The genes of an embryo are influenced by the parents and their perceptions and beliefs, satisfying what it known as genetic determinism. But when a child is born, while it adapts to its environment in order to grow, it begins to develop its genes to support any new perceptions and beliefs. While the parents have great influence on the world that the child is born into, the child also brings with it its own purpose and aspects of its being that are to play a part in the evolution of its environment. This is possible because we all have the ability to change our environment and create whatever existence we can think of.

Masaru Emoto, a researcher and author, contributed to this knowledge when he claimed that human consciousness has an effect on the molecular structure of water. He claimed that polluted water could be cleaned through prayer and positive visualization. In his experiments, he viewed ice crystals under a microscope that had been exposed to positive or negative words, pictures, and music, while in its liquid state. The crystals would react and transform into different shapes depending on the environment it was presented with, whether it was positive or negative. This is more evidence that our environment can be manipulated and is manipulated every day to support our perceived reality. It is evidence to the fact that we are the creators of our environment.

Thomas Campbell, a former NASA physicist and author of the book *My Big TOE,* concluded that "The bottom line is that the larger consciousness system is designed and constructed to support your personal growth in any way that could possibly be effective for you. It will not help you experience things that are likely to increase your entropy—you do enough of that yourself."

ACTIONS AND REACTIONS

We are now aware of the fact that our thoughts create our reality. It's a powerful fact, if you think about it. However, we lose sight of its truth and essence when we use it for our desires.

When you act on desire, when you seek love, satisfaction, happiness, or any other emotional state, you separate yourself from your natural, unconflicted, state and are setting yourself up for imbalance. Like Newton's Third Law of Motion explains, for every action there's an equal and opposite reaction. By you seeking, you put the opposite into action. Take love, for example. It is common that people only find love when they stop looking for it or don't want it at all. This law follows the same idea. Movement is a great example of how this principle can be explained. Any force that creates movement will create an opposing force that counters its movement. In order for something to move in any direction, there must be something that was stationary to move in the opposite direction of the movement created. A stone dropped to the ground will create an opposing force in the air to counter its fall and the stone will drop to the ground. All actions are one with its reaction and always complementary to each other. Morihei Ueshiba developed a Japanese martial arts technique called Aikido based on this philosophy in which a defender redirects momentum created by an opponent's attack to protect them from injury. Knowing that an action will always produce an equal and opposite reaction has been vital to science. It's one we must consider when we observe our own thoughts and actions.

SPIRITUALITY

Spirituality is the realm that encompasses all pursuits to attain a higher state of consciousness with the purpose of realizing one's divine nature and connection to all things. Other realms may pursue a similar goal, but spiritual quests are unique in the way that they are individual and personal. The answers that one receives come from oneself and the internalization of their experiences as opposed to the experiences mentioned in an established doctrine. Also, another factor that constitutes a journey being spiritual is that one embarks on it with the intention to receive reward and fulfillment in one's present life as opposed to the next or afterlife.

Some primary practices and realms of belief within spirituality include: New Age, Psychotherapy, hallucinogenic drugs, Wicca, Shamanism, breath work, yoga, holistic medicine, as well as the esoteric teachings within religions such as Gnosticism and Kabbalah, among others. Essentially, it's anything that someone engages in with the intention and goal to improve, awaken, or become enlightened.

According to the French philosopher Pierre Teilhard de Chardin, "We are not human beings having a spiritual experience; we are spiritual beings having a human experience."

THE CORE OF WHO WE ARE

So who are we really? What does being a "spiritual being" mean? The story that I think explains it perfectly is one that was inspired by esoteric Hindu beliefs.

It all started with Brahma, the ineffable, indescribable, force that created the universe. He created the void and space. He created the world. However, because of his divine nature, Brahma could not experience the world he created. He wanted to experience his creation and immerse himself in it, but simply couldn't from the confines of his divine existence. So he created Maya, the Goddess of Illusion. When Maya was brought into existence, she influenced Brahma into creating all living things: organisms, animals, plants, water, air and ether. But Brahma was still unable to experience his own creation because he could not physically play and interact with it. So then, Maya told him to create humans. When he did, Brahma was able to observe them interacting with the world but was still not able to himself. Maya, realizing what was needed, cut Brahma into tiny pieces and put a part of him into every human. Humans, in order to fully engage in the world as a finite being, could not know they had that piece of Brahma in them, but were to spend their entire existences endeavoring to discover that truth, one experience at a time. Or they would continue living in an illusion. Having that choice was part of the grand drama that was created by Brahma and Maya's union. It was a choice that would echo in life to the very end.

In this existence, humans live in a state that perpetuates the illusion until one awakens to their true nature and realizes their reality is of their own creation. The ultimate objective, and the way for the show to end, is for all conscious beings to go behind the curtain, for all of us to open our eyes and live in the world knowing we all come from the same source, that we're all one and we are God. Still, as we know, most of the time, the illusion seems to only get stronger and we drift further apart from finding our divinity.

This illusion we live in, the reason it still exists and evolves, is due to the mask that keeps our eyes veiled from seeing the truth: our ego. In spirituality, the ego has an even greater purpose than what we discussed with the human mind. Not only does it make decisions, but it also serves as the veil that dictates the existence of those decisions in the first place. The ego is a mask that we placed on ourselves so that we could become a participant in this reality. Our ego is Maya manifested into our minds. It is what allows us to interact and engage with this world fully, with vigor and emotion. I mean, imagine, how boring would our lives be if we knew our divine nature? What if we had absolutely no limitations? One would be Midas in this illusion and be unable to interact with anything for they would have no limitations or attachments and, therefore, no experiences. Think about it. Try to imagine a limitless, omniscient, omnipotent and all-knowing divine God engaging in this reality and connecting with the people, places, and things around it. Having limitations and attachments is what allows us to experience this illusion that is comprised of programmed beliefs, opinions, judgments, and feelings.

And all of our egos are different, customized to the environment we are to experience in this incarnation—decorated with a variation of the treacheries we're to endure. But while they are all different, they exist for the same purpose: to limit us so that we may remain enthralled and blind to the fact that the world is an illusion. It keeps us in the illusion, preventing us from even questioning any other possibility. And it serves its purpose well. But, remember, our egos were ultimately meant to be overcome. While you have the choice to hold fast to the illusory existence—there's nothing wrong with that—at some point you will come to realize and accept the one factor that holds true for all: you are a spiritual, divine, being.

THE SHELL KNOWN AS YOUR BODY

One of the things that most defines us humans are our individual bodies. Our bodies are the basics of the illusion, for it is our bodies that are responsible for our next steps—the things we do, the foods we eat, the places we go, ultimately, even, how long we are on Earth for until we die.

In the spiritual realm and its understandings, your body is a metaphor. It is a metaphor for all of the emotions you are storing. More specifically, it contains all of your unresolved issues that are in need of healing and resolution. So, for example, when your throat hurts, that means there is something regarding communication that needs to be resolved. Or, let's say, there's discomfort or pain in your heart. You may be repressing or experiencing feelings of love that are in need of your attention. Essentially, your body is a list of all of the things you are meant to experience in this life. The sensations of discomfort you feel within your body are the means for how you become aware of them. Even if you are not aware of some of your body's discomfort, your subconscious may be storing attached emotions of an experience that hasn't been released.

All experiences are without emotions, naturally. But, your perceptions can allow you to infuse an emotion into the experience, creating an imbalance. When you carry this imbalance, it becomes a "debt" that must be paid. Your body then stores that imbalance, that debt, inside your body's energy field, wherever it resonates, leading to the sensation or discomfort you experience. Energy healers are great at helping you transform and release those energies, just as well as a medical doctor or psychotherapist can get you to release that ingrained belief that you are sick. However, there is only one true healer and it's you! Someone who doesn't understand this will continue struggling to try and heal, never achieving it and never returning to balance. Remember, you're the only one doing the healing—no one else. As stated simply in *A Course in Miracles*, "A patient decides that it is so, and he recovers. If he decides against recovery, he will not be healed. Who is the physician? Only the mind of the patient himself. The outcome is what he decides that it is."

I will explain further with the example of a SCUBA diver. When diving at lower underwater depths, a diver is susceptible to lack of oxygen in their bloodstream, known as Hypoxia. The only way to relieve this imbalance is to shrink any gas bubbles formed during ascent by infusing oxygen back into their bloodstream using various methods and techniques. When available, a hyperbaric chamber is normally used to bring the diver's environment to a balanced level through the use of pure oxygen. We are all susceptible to becoming imbalanced, but as long as we are able to become aware of it we are then able to heal and get back in balance.

Balance can only be achieved by releasing our emotional attachment to an experience. We naturally infuse some form of emotional energy to all our experiences, such as when we go to a movie theater to watch a funny movie and we laugh. There is an investment made by you in the experience and sometimes we are unable to release it so it gets stored as a debt and imbalance until you're ready to release it.

The concept of the body as a metaphor, one that can be empowered by thought, can be especially seen in those that have debilitating behaviors, such as addicts. Typically, anyone who suffers from any type of addiction and wishes to stop has a very difficult time doing so. Usually, this leads them to seek help, like at a rehabilitation center. But no one can stop this addictive behavior except the person who created the addiction in the first place. For that is what it is at its most basic level—a creation. There is more anecdotal evidence proving the benefits of those that abruptly stop their addictive behavior as opposed to those who go to clinics or seek help from health professionals in a long protracted cleansing process. This is because they eliminated the hardest part of rehab—they've eliminated the emotional conflict. By not infusing any thought into the process and releasing the behavior, the addiction is no longer there. This may be a rudimentary explanation of how habits can be broken. But know that rehabilitation can only be achieved through the will and strength of the addict himself.

PURPOSE FOR INCARNATION

Knowing what I know, I have asked myself many times what would be the reason to incarnate into this world. If we are all supreme, all-powerful, beings capable of the magnificence of creation itself, what's the point of becoming human? The truth is, while it is an illusion, this world allows us to experience a plethora of emotions that would be impossible otherwise. In this world, we experience love, hate, happiness, sadness, friendships, fear, courage, sickness, health, life, death, and everything in between. It seems that this is an experience of limitations that we were meant to have as a small semblance of our collective existence, allowing ourselves to evolve until we all understand our divine nature. And the only way to achieve it, is to incarnate here as an intelligent being capable of reasoning, gain experience, and ultimately remember that we are all God because we all come from God. This is an awareness that escaped us amidst the experience.

We were born knowing our divine nature, but very quickly began to realize that in order to play in this reality we would have to wear a mask. The mask is the mechanism by which we interact with all experiences and get caught up in the emotional states that we create. Our mistake is forgetting that we have a mask on. If we are to realize our divine nature and bring harmony to our life, we will first have to remind ourselves that we have a mask on and then become aware of it in all of our experiences. This awareness allows us to have a more harmonious interaction with all experiences without creating any imbalance.

Reincarnation is a concept explaining that we may have lived other lives or need to in order to experience all there is until we reach enlightenment or ascension. But it isn't necessary. There is no true use in thinking of a past life. What you are really accessing is the power of the collective consciousness. Everything is there for you to experience, right now. So do it and know that everything in your life, every experience, has its reason and its lesson. This includes the work you do, the friends you have, your possessions and, most importantly, your family. The things you don't like in your life are the things you're meant to overcome. Your perception of the things around you, of everything that is outside of you, is a reflection of who you are inside. It is a reflection of everything that you are to ultimately let go of in order to become aware of and live harmoniously with your true nature.

PART FOUR

HARMONY

TRANSFORMATION

By questioning all that we've learned, all that we've investigated, and becoming aware of the knowledge within us, we transform. True transformation is achieving the awareness that the truth we've been seeking has been with us since the start. We never needed to search for anything, we just needed to open our eyes and let go of the illusion.

At the stage you are right now, you do not require a guru, teacher, yogi, prophet, preacher, mentor, or rabbi to tell you how to achieve this transformation. You just need to let go. Meditation, praying, yoga, sitting on a rock in the desert, or any other form that connects you to nature and the outside world, is not required. Again, you just need to let go. You are the only source of conflict, the only thing standing in the way. You are your ultimate roadblock on the path to self-realization.

HOW IS CONFLICT CREATED?

Conflict is created the second we seek something, or emotionally attach ourselves to an experience. Desire and attachment create conflict. Trusting in something we haven't questioned also creates conflict.

BLIND FAITH

Blind faith is an unconventional means to guide oneself through life using untested and unquestioned beliefs. These beliefs serve only to keep our minds enslaved in someone else's reality. Thomas Campbell said, "That a million smart people say 'yes' is not a good reason for you to say 'yes' if you do not have the experience and understanding to support it. Determining truth is not a democratic process ruled by the majority. It is also not something that someone else can do for you. Do not let these smart people sway you to agree with them simply because they are smart." When we give faith, it must be questioned and examined. Failure to test our faith will ensure that we continue being slaves to whatever we have invested our faith in.

When circus elephants are babies, they are tied to a metal stake on the ground using a very strong chain. The baby elephants try to escape, but soon realize that their attempts are futile, and painful, which causes them to cease their attempts. This keeps them obedient. When the elephant becomes fully grown, sometimes weighing 13,000 pounds, they are tied to the ground using a wooden peg and a flimsy chain. This full sized elephant is capable of breaking away easily, but because his mind has conditioned itself to believe that his attempts are futile, he doesn't even try to escape. Inevitably, he succumbs to the limitations of his own thoughts. As Thomas Campbell also said, "A man who will not leave his room because he does not know how or is afraid to open the door is trapped just the same whether or not the door is locked."

If we let our beliefs govern our life, we are limited by the convention of others, and we would no longer exercise our ability to question our beliefs in order to understand their correlation to our lives and the experiences they create. We would be doing ourselves a disservice because we would continue to live in a perpetual state of disharmony.

To live with sight, and not follow blindly, we must realize that this is all just a show, an act. And then we must keep acting. But we must not believe the mask we are wearing and the beliefs it's filled with. Believing that our mask, and the role we are playing, is who we really are will keep us blind to the truth.

We must become aware and observe our world in an objective manner, questioning everything and discerning its purpose as either a lesson or experience. Everything that happens in our lives serves a purpose and we must never think otherwise.

Let's start believing in ourselves and our capacity to have the most amazing life. Know that we can continue performing in this great play even if we awaken. And we are not to judge those that wish to continue living in the illusion, that is their choice and could even be the role they are to portray now. However, if we are to live a life without conflict to our natural state, then we must be in harmony with ourselves. And realizing that this is one great show is part of that. Those who preach otherwise, and convince us otherwise, will keep us blind. We must not fall prey to old conventions. May we continue to acknowledge our mind's role in all aspects of our lives.

As we discussed earlier, a mind that believes it is sick will inevitably activate the respective cells to create a sickness in its body. Nothing can exist in our bodies that our mind has not invited in. Lisa Rankin M.D. wrote in Psychology Today about the phenomenon of the nocebo effect. "Patients about to undergo surgery who were 'convinced' of their impending death were compared to another group of patients who were merely "unusually apprehensive" about death. While the apprehensive bunch fared pretty well, those who were convinced they were going to die usually did. Similarly, women who believed they were prone to heart disease were four times more likely to die. It's not because these women had poorer diets, higher blood pressure, higher cholesterol, or stronger family histories than the women who didn't get heart disease. The only difference between the two groups was their beliefs."

The above example explains it quite simply. We have been conditioned to trust people because we believe they know more than we do, we believe their role in the show is means for complete trust. But it's only when we question that trust that we will see past the surface of their role and realize they have the same power we do, nothing beyond that. We are governors of our own bodies and our minds are the creators of our reality. Nothing happens unless you want it to happen—nothing.

Blame genetics, your environment, or your actions, and you will continue to live in a reality that perpetuates that. You will live in conflict and disharmony. This is how we've been living up to now. But we can transcend that way of thinking, let go of the emotions attached to our experiences, look at the dualistic harmony in which we are presented with, and find the divine beauty and purpose of our lives.

In the Bhagavad Gita written around 400 BCE, Lord Krishna said, "A man consists of his faith, and as his faith is, so is he." This is very true. Take Tarzan, for example. Although fictional, his story is a great example. Tarzan was a young British boy whose parents died after being marooned on the coast of Africa, became orphaned and was raised by apes in the African jungles. The child grew to believe he was an ape and did everything as if he were one. Years passed and Tarzan became a young adult. He was then found by a search party and brought back to civilization. Tarzan quickly learned that he was unable to adapt to a civilized society and went back to the African jungles to rejoin his ape "family." His belief in his inability to adapt to a new environment is what drove him back, nothing else.

We are the products of our environment, beliefs, culture, heritage and other factors that are apparent in our lives. But we are not ultimately bound by them if we don't want to be. We can transcend. But the core of your being is concentrated on how you perceive yourself. Keep thinking you are an ape and you will remain one.

HOW TO RELEASE CONFLICT

As discussed previously, it is imperative that we let go of the past and the beliefs that no longer serve us. Letting go is the most significant step in transforming and achieving self-realization. Thus, it is my goal to help you release anything and everything that does not serve you, right now. For this, we're going to use an exercise inspired by Robert Scheinfeld's process for releasing emotion. This moment is for you. Take the time to fully commit to the following exercise and see how it transforms your way of thinking. Notice how you begin to see things a little bit differently. Do it for one experience, do it for all. Just do it.

Start by searching your mind and picking an experience, a vivid one. The experience you choose, whether positive or negative, is of no consequence. Then, follow these steps:

1. Before you go in, remind yourself that the experience and the emotions connected to it are not real.

2. Make the image of the experience as lucid as possible. Immerse yourself in it. Focus on the colors, the sounds, and the textures, if any. How do you feel? Point at the emotion you're feeling, open it up and expose it.

3. Feel the energy fully. Allow the feeling to reach its peak, then speak to the feeling and call it what it is. Tell the truth.

4. Reclaim your power from the creation.

5. Now release. Let go of the emotion.

6. Appreciate the experience.

BECOME THE OBSERVER

Things are going to happen in our lives, and we're going to feel a range of emotions. It's all part of the human experience. But there is something wonderful that happens when we become the observer and witness those events as they are happening.

As aware and awake individuals, we are no longer experiencing life mindlessly but consciously witnessing the different factors at play in each moment. And with this awareness, we can give in to an emotion but then just as easily choose to refrain from it. It allows us to choose our next move, mindfully. It allows us to choose, period.

Let's say you're engaging in a conversation with someone and they make a statement that you don't agree with. First and foremost, you must realize that, by you not agreeing with them, you have created an opinion and infused an emotion into the belief that has been presented to you. Then, after you acknowledge the judgment, take a step back in your mind. You are not there to go against them. Instead, allow that other person to present their entire argument to you without your interjection. Don't argue with them. Simply acknowledge that the argument they are presenting is their perspective and only a piece of information, one piece of the story. That's it. Just let the conversation play itself out. Observe it in its wonderful entirety. If you respond, know that you will only be serving your ego. Do the above and you will have been the observer of your reality. If you had interjected, again, knowing what you know now, you would have made a conscious decision to act. And should that decision have been to prove them wrong, let's say, you would have created karma and conflict.

Those that voice an opinion, have an objective. An observer has no opinion. An observer instead acknowledges that the other person is but a part of themselves, there to reveal an alternate perspective of a certain topic. It's all to reveal the topic to you as a whole, to reveal yourself to you as a whole. Next time you find yourself in such a situation, verbally agree with them and, in turn, you will have helped reveal that person and their perspective to themselves, and you will have diverted conflict.

Being an observer can be somewhat difficult, but with some measure of restraint you may find that those kinds of experiences will begin to dissipate and other experiences will materialize.

THE NATURAL STATE

The Natural State is the state in which there is no conflict or desire. It neither has nor supports duality, it just knows that all aspects of the concept will complement each other. The divine self doesn't see polarity. It sees the beauty in all sides of an event as one whole picture. It sees one grand show.

In practice, however, to live in the natural state is to acknowledge that conflict will arise and, when it does, a means to attain balance will be recognized and achieved.

All of us have some sort of beliefs and in those beliefs are untethered emotions that have kept us in karmic debt. As we are all addicted to emotions, it is what has validated our experiences so that we conform to societal norms. Our addiction has allowed us to infuse those emotions into our experiences to make the experiences appear more real. But we know now that it's not real. The only recovery from this addiction is to first acknowledge our emotions, release those emotions, then reclaim the energy we gave those emotions, and finally thank the emotions for the lessons they taught us.

The natural state is a state of balance where you can play with an emotion in an experience but not dwell in it. Our free will is what allows us to do this. This may be difficult to understand and realize, at first, which is why it is important to really focus and practice making observations. Notice when you're feeling an emotion, or several, throughout an experience and just allow that experience to happen without interruption. The more you consciously practice observing, the quicker it will become basic instinct. Observing will become natural to you, an unconscious behavior. You will recognize your ability to have any emotional experience without any attachment to the experience. Then, play as you wish. But never forget, life is one big performance. And it's just an illusion.

CONCLUSION

There is no doubt that you now know what's within you. At the very least, you've begun to graze the surface and are on your way to further discovery. We've discussed the essence of who we are, where we came from, and what we are doing here. More specifically, we've discussed the truth that God is within all of us, God is all of us, and we are all pieces of the one great God.

We were all created by the primal thought known as the Creation. That thought, and all thoughts since, created the reality we live in. All thoughts from here after, then, shall create our futures. We are in charge, consciously in charge, of what happens from here on out.

We also have a sense now of how we're all related and here to help each other. So every experience has a purpose. Let's be the observer and see what is really happening in our experiences. Let's be one with ourselves and act in our nature so that we move forward without creating conflict and karma. Let's evolve in harmony. Now that we have questioned what we've learned in the past and have come to a realization of who we truly are, we can recognize and live in our natural state. We can move on. And we can perform as we were intended.

In ancient Greek, the word for "acting" was *hypokrisis*, as in our modern day word "hypocrite," and meant to speak or to act under a false part. We are all actors performing our role and interacting with each other blinded by the truth of our divine nature. As we awaken, we reveal to ourselves how intricate this play really is. And we are able to observe how our emotions are used to attach ourselves to all of our experiences. There's nothing wrong with this awakening, just as there's nothing wrong with us being asleep. There's nothing wrong with remaining in the dream and discarding the contents of this book. It's up to each and every one of us what happens from now on.

The Hindu Trimurti, the supreme divinity composed of Brahma the Creator, Vishnu the Preserver, and Shiva the Destroyer, foretells the effects of what happens next. Think of our old beliefs. They were born, we preserved them, and now we're slowly destroying them. We are born, we live, and then we die. And so will this be with our world. It was born, it's preserved, it will ultimately be destroyed.

We'll see how long it lasts. In the meantime, enjoy what you've created.

REFERENCES

"Formal Results: Testing the GCP Hypothesis."
Global Consciousness Project. 1998-2015.
http://noosphere.princeton.edu/results.html.

"Native Spirituality according to Luther Standing
Bear." 2008.
http://mendotadakota.com/mn/native-
spirituality-according-to-luther-standing-
bear/.

"Organized religion." *Wikipedia.*
https://en.wikipedia.org/wiki/Organized_reli
gion.

"Religion." *Merriam-Webster.*
https://www.merriam-
webster.com/dictionary/religion?utm_campa
ign=sd&utm_medium=serp&utm_source=js
onld.

"Religion." *Dictionary.com.*
http://www.dictionary.com/browse/religion.

"Science." *Dictionary.com.*
http://www.dictionary.com/browse/science.

"Science." *Cambridge Dictionary.*
http://dictionary.cambridge.org/us/dictionary
/english/science.

"Socrates." *New World Encyclopedia.*
http://www.newworldencyclopedia.org/entry
/Socrates.

"The Second Noble Truth: The Noble Truth of the
Origin of dukkha." *Access to Insight.* 2013.
http://www.accesstoinsight.org/ptf/dhamma/
sacca/sacca2/index.html.

"What does the Bible say about how to find purpose
in life?" *GotQuestions.org.*
https://www.gotquestions.org/purpose-of-
life.html.

"What is the Global Consciousness Project?"
Global Consciousness Project. 1998-2015.
http://noosphere.princeton.edu/introduction.
html.

Amundson, Ron. "The Hundredth Monkey
Phenomenon." 1985.
https://hilo.hawaii.edu/~ronald/HMP.htm.

Bhagavad-Gita Trust. "Chapter 17, Verse 3."
http://www.bhagavad-gita.org/Gita/verse-
17-03.html.

Bhikkhu, Thanissaro. "Kalama Sutta: To the
Kalamas.
http://www.accesstoinsight.org/tipitaka/an/a
n03/an03.065.than.html.

Bodh, Bhikkhu. "The Noble Eightfold Path: The Way to the End of Suffering." *Access to Insight*. 2013. http://www.accesstoinsight.org/lib/authors/bodhi/waytoend.html.

Campbell, Thomas. *My Big TOE: The Complete Trilogy.* Lightning Strike books, 2007.

Campbell, Thomas. *My Big Toe.* https://www.my-big-toe.com/

Dumoulin, Heinrich. *Zen Buddhism: A History, India & China.* World Wisdom, 2005.

Fisher, David James. *Romain Rolland and the Politics of Intellectual Engagement.* Berkeley: University of California Press, 1988.

Meshberger, Frank Lynn. "An Interpretation of Michelangelo's Creation of Adam Based on Neuroanatomy." *JAMA: The Journal of the American Medical Association* 264, no. 14 (October 1990): 1838-1841.

Baker, Robert J., and Ronald K. Chesser. "The Chernobyl Nuclear Disaster and Subsequent Creation of a Wildlife Preserve." *Environmental Toxicology and Chemistry* 19, no. 5 (2000): 1231-1232. http://www.nsrl.ttu.edu/chornobyl/wildlifepreserve.htm

Lamb, Robert. "What is the anthropic principle?" 2010. *HowStuffWorks*. http://science.howstuffworks.com/science-vs-myth/everyday-myths/anthropic-principle.htm.

Lavine, T.Z. *From Socrates to Sartre: The Philosophic Quest.* Bantam, 1985.

Lipton, Bruce H. *The Biology of Belief: Unleashing the Power of Consciousness, Matter, & Miracles.* Hay House, 2008.

M.D., Lisa Rankin. "The Nocebo Effect: Negative Thoughts Can Harm Your Health." *Psychology Today.* 2013. https://www.psychologytoday.com/blog/owning-pink/201308/the-nocebo-effect-negative-thoughts-can-harm-your-health.

Miller, Barbara Stoler. *The Bhagavad-Gita: Krishna's Counsel In Time of War*. QPBC, 1998.

Freedman, Rabbi Dr. H. and Maurice Simon. "Midrash Rabbah: Translated Into English." https://archive.org/stream/RabbaGenesis/midrashrabbahgen027557mbp_djvu.txt

Rovelli, Carlo. "Relational quantum mechanics." *International Journal of Theoretical Physics* 35, no. 8 (1996): 1637–1678.

Schucman, Helen. *A Course In Miracles*. Course in Miracles Society, 1972.

Ueshiba, Morihei. *The Art of Peace.* Shambhala, 2002.

"Backgrounder on Chernobyl Nuclear Power Plant Accident." *USNRC*. 2014. https://www.nrc.gov/reading-rm/doc-collections/fact-sheets/chernobyl-bg.html.

Waddington, C. H. *The Strategy of the Genes: A Discussion of Some Aspects of Theoretical Biology.* George Allen & Unwin, 1957.

"What is the Photograph of Frozen Water Crystals?" *Masaru Emoto*. 2010. http://www.masaru-emoto.net/english/water-crystal.html.

Jones, Judy, and William Wilson. *An Incomplete Education.* Ballantine Books, 2008.

"Word Study: Ezer Kenegdo." *God's Word to Women.* https://godswordtowomen.org/ezerkenegdo.htm.

Weiten, Wayne. *Psychology: Themes and Variations.* Thomson Wadworth, 2007.

ABOUT ME

While I regularly attended Catholic service growing up, I was never truly interested in following any organized religion. Although, I did briefly study Buddhism, Hinduism, Gnosticism, and further looked into Christianity. Still, I never found what I was looking for. During my late 40s, I began to question everything I knew and believed. I came to the realization that my existence was defined through concepts that I did not personally discover, but was taught. My "aha" moment came when I began questioning my beliefs about "God." The concept of "God" being an outside force that created, and continued to control, everything around me was a trigger. This belief could not be supported when I began to question the fundamentals of what

I understood, so I dropped the belief and came to the realization that "God" was actually inside of me and that there was no need to search—for anything. I realized that the puzzle and mystery of our existence was defined by taking responsibility for everything that was happening in our lives. And once I accepted this, I would acknowledge that I was the only power capable of creating my experiences. I realized that I was a creator. That's when my life changed. That's when I found peace. Ultimately, that was my hope in writing this book: to offer the opportunity for others to find harmony in their lives and live their true purpose, and to find peace.

www.ingramcontent.com/pod-product-compliance
Lightning Source LLC
Chambersburg PA
CBHW031623040426
42452CB00007B/651